THE NEW TEAMWORK

DEVELOPING AND USING CROSS-FUNCTION TEAMS

Marshall Sashkin and Molly G. Sashkin

AMA Management Briefing

AMA MEMBERSHIP PUBLICATIONS DIVISION
AMERICAN MANAGEMENT ASSOCIATION

For information on how to order additional copies of this publication, see page 85.

Library of Congress Cataloging-in-Publication Data

Sashkin, Marshall, 1944–
  The new teamwork : developing and using cross-function teams /
Marshall Sashkin and Molly G. Sashkin.
    p.   cm.—(AMA management briefing)
  ISBN 0-8144-2353-1
  1. Work groups.   I. Sashkin, Molly G.   II. Title.   III. Series.
HD66.S27   1994
658.4'02—dc20   *94-2165*
                    3 2280 00477 1002   *CIP*

This Management Briefing has been distributed to all members enrolled in the American Management Association.

First printing.

Contents

Preface

As we approach a new century and millennium, we see the pace of the movement to team-based organization accelerating. This is happening despite the warnings of a few vocal reactionaries who wish for the security of hierarchical authority, or who dream of simpler times when almost all work achievements were based on the determined efforts of individuals. Even so, the Luddites of the latter twentieth century are no more likely to change the course of this new development than were their counterparts of an earlier time.

And yet there are real problems to be faced and overcome. The sort of team approach characteristic of the past decade (and increasingly characteristic of organizations of the 1990s) is in some important ways ill-suited to the continuing developments in organization and technology. More and more, teams cannot afford to be highly autonomous and independent one of another. The limits and dangers to "semi-autonomy" are becoming more evident; work teams must of necessity find new ways to coordinate, not just in standardized ways *between* two teams, but in complex and uncertain ways *among* teams and functions in varied parts of the organization.

We believe that there are some important lessons to be

learned, not just from the successes but from the problems faced and, sometimes, overcome by teams as organizations struggle with these new demands and the problems they create. Other learning derives from the newly rediscovered area of quality, perhaps best illustrated by the work of W. Edwards Deming, Joseph M. Juran, and others who developed the foundations for "total quality management."

In this briefing, we draw on the work of classical organizational theorists like Max Weber, modern organizational scientists such as Rensis Likert, and dedicated practitioners like Deming and Juran. Our purpose is to trace the development of the team approach in organizations, to understand why it has been so successful, and to identify the sort of further changes that will be required if the team structures of the 1980s and 1990s are to work effectively in the cross-functionally integrated organizations of the next century.

We are also committed to identifying and describing some of the most important tools, techniques, and development methods that can assist in making the changes and meeting the challenges required in the coming decades. Because this is a brief introduction, we can hardly claim to provide comprehensive instructions; in every case we suggest key reference resources for those who wish to go beyond understanding to action.

We have drawn heavily on the work of great social and organizational scientists of the past. While it may not be as evident, we have drawn equally on the recent and continuing work of colleagues engaged in understanding and changing organizations in ways better suited to the demands of a changing social, technological, and economic environment. We have been deeply influenced by the work of our friend and mentor Warren Bennis, by the work on team-based organizations of Edward E. Lawler III and his colleagues, by the socio-technical ideas and ideals of the late Eric Trist, and by the team approach conceived and taught by our first mentor, Norman R. F. Maier. And we have used freely the fundamental yet pragmatic ideas developed by W. Edwards Deming. To all of these and the many others on whose work this briefing is based we offer our sincere thanks, recognizing that while we may attempt to share the credit, responsibility for all of the arguments presented here remains solely our own. We cannot, however, conclude without offering our greatest appreciation to our friend and editor Don Bohl, without whose constant support and encouragement this project would not have come to fruition. His assistance, both technical and conceptual, has greatly improved and strengthened this briefing.

We hope that this briefing proves useful as well as interesting, and that it provokes questions and actions of the sort crucial for the continued development of team-based organizations. It is our firm conviction that the organizations we describe here will prove not only to be more economically viable (as compared with the types of organization they replace), but also better places for people. Our presentation will have succeeded if, after reading this briefing, you agree.

Introduction

Teams and teamwork have become such a common part of management and organizations that we often take their need and usefulness for granted. As we will see, this was not always true. There was a time when a work team was little more than a number of people each doing a similar task or even just pulling on the same rope, and thus combining efforts to achieve what could not be done by one person. But it takes more than a bunch of people pulling on the same rope to make a team.

In Chapter One and Chapter Two, we show why and how teams became so important in organizations. Chapter Three takes us further, to explore why the basic team is no longer enough, why we must go beyond simple work teams to create and develop "cross-function" teams.

The cross-function team (as described in Chapter Four) is simply a group of people who come from (and often represent) different parts of an organization. Such teams are often temporary, that is, they are formed to deal with a special problem or complete a specific task. Other cross-function teams are more than temporary task forces; they go on indefinitely, to deal with recurring problems or an ongoing task mission.

Individual cross-function team members may keep their

formal "identity" as part of a "home" group, unit, team, or department while they are assigned temporarily to the cross-function team. Or they may be more or less permanently assigned to a cross-function team, and their identity as a member of this unit gradually replaces affiliation with the function from which they were drawn.

Cross-function teams exist because they represent a new and proven way of dealing more effectively with organizational problems and challenges. These issues may involve outside problems, such as competition, technological change, or government regulation. Or they may develop from within the organization and center on problems of coordinating the design, development, manufacture, and marketing of a product. The diversity of the team members supports collaborative and creative work efforts. The central advantage of a cross-function team is that it brings together information, knowledge, and skills that might not otherwise be readily available. By design, the information, knowledge, and skills the cross-function team can draw on are crucial for the effective resolution of complex problems involving technology and the coordinated development of a product or service.

Of course, cross-function teams also present challenges. In an ordinary team, people often have problems and conflicts. It's not always easy to reconcile what one person wants with the views of another. This issue is an even more common problem for cross-function teams. The structure of such teams makes it likely that some conflict among team members will be a continual challenge to the smooth operation of the team. Conflict is, however, neither good nor bad in and of itself. It's how one *uses* conflicts, either to spur creativity in a win-win mode, or to play factions one against another in a zero-sum/win-lose manner, that makes conflict "good" or "bad."

The challenge of cross-function teams is to learn to use conflict in positive and productive ways. In Part II of this briefing, we will describe a variety of tools and development techniques that cross-function teams can use to meet the challenge of integrating diverse views and finding creative ways to resolve differences. As cross-function teams become more common, perhaps even a basic characteristic of twenty-first century organizations, we may well find it puzzling that the questions and issues discussed in this briefing even needed to be addressed. At some point in the future, it may be as odd to think of organizations without cross-function teams as it is today to think of organizations without teams and teamwork.

Part I

How Did We Get Here?

This part of the briefing tells the story of the Lobo & Tiburon Toy Company, a fictional organization based loosely on a classic case study in teamwork and organizational change.

In Chapter One, we use this story as a platform for examining why teams are useful and necessary in organizations. In Chapters Two and Three, we use the toymaker narrative to show how the concept of teams has evolved over time. In particular, we look at the way that teams depend on one another and what consequences such "interdependencies" have for the organization. Finally, in Chapter Four, we return to Lobo & Tiburon to demonstrate how social and organizational changes require a new sort of team, a team that to be effective must work *smarter* (but not necessarily *harder*) than ever before.

1

The Toymaker

The Lobo & Tiburon Company[1] manufactured wooden toys of various kinds: wooden animals, dolls, pull toys, etc. It all started in the wood room, where employees cut, sanded, and partly assembled wooden parts. They then dipped the parts into shellac and sent them to the paint room, where other workers sprayed paint on the partially assembled toys in preparation for the drying oven. The company's toys were mostly two-colored, although some were three- and a few four-colored; each color required a separate trip through the oven.

Management had recently reengineered the entire painting process. The eight workers now sat in a line alongside an endless chain of hooks that passed by at eye-level as they traveled into the long, horizontal drying oven. Each worker sat at a paint booth that was ventilated to carry away fumes. He or she would take a toy part from a tray, position it on a holder

[1]The Lobo & Tiburon Toy Company case is a synthesis of information from several cases and sources. In particular, we draw on material from the Hovey and Beard case, which was originally prepared by George Strauss from information provided by Alex Bavelas and published in *Money and Motivation* by William Foote Whyte (New York: Harper & Row, 1955). The L&T Toy Company is not intended to represent any actual organization, nor does this briefing actually describe what happened at Hovey and Beard.

inside the cubicle, spray on the color according to a pattern, and then hang the part on a passing hook.

Engineers had calculated the rate at which the hooks moved so that workers would be able to hang a painted toy part on each hook before it passed out of reach. This ensured that every hook would be filled as it entered the oven.

The toy painters were on a group bonus plan. Since the operation was new to them, they received a special learning bonus that decreased by a set amount each month. The learning bonus was designed to disappear after six months, by which time the painters were expected to be able to meet the standard. If they exceeded it, they would earn a bonus.

Because the workers had been trained together and seemed to enjoy each others' company, management was confident that a team spirit would develop. And the bonus would re-enforce that sense of teamwork. All in all, management saw the reengineered work flow as a model plan.

Troubles in Toyland

By the second month following the reengineering, trouble developed. The painters were learning very slowly; management began to suspect their production would always be well below the desired level. Many hooks went into the oven empty—even so, the workers complained that the hooks were going too fast, and charged that the speed had been set wrong. A few painters quit and had to be replaced with new employees, which further aggravated the learning problem. Except for the complaints team members shared, the team spirit that management had expected from the group was nonexistent.

One worker (the group regarded her as its leader, management as its ringleader) was outspoken. She hurled the sort of complaints one would expect when workers are generally frustrated: the job was too messy, the hooks moved too fast, the incentive wasn't being calculated correctly, the room was too hot, and so on. In sum, the operation was plagued by absenteeism, turnover, and low morale.

Clearly, something had to be done. But before we continue the story, we need to look at the kind of thinking that led the engineers at Lobo & Tiburon to design the work as they did.

WHAT IS A TEAM?

What sort of a "team" was operating at the L&T Company? Is it really accurate to refer to the painters as a "team" when each person was working alone on a sort of modified assembly line? In fact, the arrangement we've described is little more than an assembly-line-like mechanization of what is still individual work. In theory, of course, this arrangement should lead to an increase in efficiency and productivity, just as the automobile assembly line dramatically increased productivity and reduced costs.

More specifically, Henry Ford's development of the auto assembly line was an example of maximum task specialization—narrowing down work tasks to their smallest physical elements. Such task design is a logical outgrowth of the work of Frederick Winslow Taylor, the "father of scientific management." Taylor, an engineer who worked in the latter part of the nineteenth and the early twentieth centuries, believed that managers could find the "one best way" to do a job—even a job as simple as shoveling coal—by breaking it down into its component parts and identifying the most efficient way to do each part. They could then teach workers to do the job the best way, step-by-step.

Henry Ford combined task specification and specialization with the notion of a moving assembly line. This new specialized-task/assembly-line design, which carefully planned every movement and action, produced a true revolution in industry. All kinds of manufacturers applied the approach. Social historians now refer to task-specialized work on an assembly line as the "second industrial revolution."

BUREAUCRACY AND ORGANIZATION

Progressive executives gradually came to apply this same approach—breaking down production tasks into specialized components—to make whole organizations more rational and controllable. In France an engineer named Henri Fayol came to head a large steel and coal organization. On the basis of his many years of experience, he concluded that in the same way that scientists use the laws of science, managers could apply a relatively small number of universal principles to operate their organizations more effectively. The concept of "chain of command," by which every person has a clearly identified supervisor, is one such principle. Fayol called it the "scalar principle." In the United States around the same time, James D. Mooney and Allen C. Reiley were advocating similar ideas.

But these notions were primitive compared with Max Weber's analysis of organization. Weber, the well-known German social scientist, coined the term "bureaucracy." In his sense of the word, bureaucracy not only implied the greatest achievable efficiency and productivity, but incorporated and supported the ideals of democracy and the protection of the worker.

Today, of course, few would associate these positive characteristics with bureaucracies, which we have come to see as wasteful and abusive, whether they are part of the private sector (General Motors, for example) or a public agency (such as the Department of Defense, which spent a small fortune developing a 30-page recipe for baking brownies). Yet in his time—the first half of this century—Weber did for large-scale organizational design what Ford did for task design: revolutionized and made more fundamentally rational what had until then been an unsystematic approach to work and organization.

As Ford and other industrialists narrowed down work tasks to their smallest physical elements and trained individual workers to perform just one or a few highly specialized operations, Weber and management theorists focused on the parallel development of organizational structures. They defined rational functions (such as personnel, finance, production, marketing, etc.) as those operated by means of a management hierarchy that uses standardized bureaucratic procedures.

The hierarchical, bureaucratic organizational form fits with the sequential assembly-line design of tasks. Both systems divide activities into the smallest possible task units, and assign individuals to one or a few such activities. They identify a "best way" to do something, then appoint individuals to do it over and over and over. The prime goal—efficiency—is achieved because employees (whether workers or managers) are able to accomplish their jobs faster by practicing the necessary skills repeatedly. Perhaps even more important, the outcomes of individuals' efforts are more certain, more reliable. After all, variability—caused by many different people doing the same thing in many different ways—is reduced or eliminated.

Concepts of bureaucracy and assembly-line efficiency have become deeply ingrained in our legacy of management thought. Thus, we should not be surprised that the L&T engineers allowed these concepts to shape their plans to the point that the paint room workers were a team in name only.

We now know that functional bureaucracy is no more the answer to every organizational problem than the assembly line is the complete solution to every productivity problem. This point became apparent to the foreman at the L&T Company.

In the next chapter, we'll look at what he did about it.

2

The Team Maker

The paint room foreman at the L&T Company was desperate for a solution to the problems of low morale and even worse production. Willing to try just about anything, he brought in a management consultant, a professor at the state university who came highly recommended. The foreman hoped the consultant would provide some new ideas and, maybe, some answers.

After meeting with the foreman, the consultant suggested that everyone—including the workers—sit down and talk. The foreman didn't think this was a great idea ("begging for trouble" was how he put it). But with no alternative, he consented. One afternoon after work, the foreman, the consultant, and all eight workers held their first team meeting.

Once again, the workers recited their complaints: the job was too dirty, the hooks moved too fast, the room was too hot, and so on. They complained most about the heat, so the foreman agreed to look into it. But after meeting with the plant engineer and his boss, the foreman became convinced that nothing could be done. Putting in air conditioning was prohibitively costly, and the plant engineer claimed there was no problem to begin with!

At the next group meeting, however, the foreman found that the workers had come up with a plan of their own. They proposed getting some big fans to circulate the air around their feet. Even though the foreman felt the idea wouldn't work, he agreed to try it. The cost was minimal and the fans could be used elsewhere if (as he expected) they did not solve the problem.

The events that followed were astonishing, at least to the foreman. The workers were not just satisfied, they were delighted. They set up the fans one way, then another way, then still another way. And regardless of the actual effects on the room's temperature, they were completely happy with the result. Morale improved.

Soon the foreman decided that group meetings weren't such a bad idea after all. He asked the workers if they might like to meet again to discuss other problems. They eagerly agreed.

More New Ideas

At the next meeting, the discussion centered on the speed of the hooks. The workers continued to insist that the speed was set unreasonably high, that they could never work as fast as the "standard" required.

Then one worker said, "It's not that I can't work that fast, it's that I just can't keep it up all day!" Soon the workers came up with another idea: Let *them* adjust the speed of the hooks. Let them speed things up or slow them down depending on how they felt. The foreman was startled, but he agreed to talk to the plant superintendent and engineers.

The engineers thought the foreman had gone crazy; but after considerable discussion and even some argument, they conceded that there was some leeway, that the speed could vary somewhat without causing more problems. They were certain that the outcome would be no change at best, and disaster at worst. Nonetheless, the plant manager gave the foreman permission to go ahead. The engineers put in a control dial marked "slow," "medium," and "fast." The speed could now be adjusted anywhere within these limits.

The Toy Team

Once again, the painters were pleased. And, for the first time, they began working the way management had hoped they would when it first instituted the group bonus arrangement.

To be sure, they spent hours discussing how to vary the speed from hour to hour, but it didn't take them long to settle on a standard pattern. The first part of the morning, the hooks moved at a speed slightly above the "medium" setting; the next two and one-half hours they moved at top speed; the half hour before and after lunch they moved at the slowest speed; and the rest of the afternoon the speed was set at maximum, except for the last 45 minutes, when it was set at medium.

The old, constant speed had been set at a little below what was now called "medium," and the workers were now operating at an average speed above the constant. So the net effect of the decision to give workers control was actually to speed up the hooks, not slow them down!

Few if any hooks now went through the oven empty, and there was no increase in defects, either. Thus, production increased. In fact, within three weeks, with the learning bonus still in effect, the workers were operating at 30 to 50 percent above the level expected under the original arrangement. They were receiving their base pay, a team piece-rate bonus, *and* the learning bonus!

Let's step aside from the story again and take a closer look at what was going on.

THE DEVELOPMENT OF TEAMWORK

Eight independent workers did not become a team just because management instituted a team-bonus incentive. But when management gave them the opportunity to act like a team, they began to do so. The foreman's experience at the L&T Company duplicates that of many executives who instituted work teams, starting as early as the 1940s. By the 1960s and 1970s, work teams had become relatively common in all types of organizations.

Teamwork design came about partly in response to the dehumanizing effects of over-specialized assembly-line work. Henry Ford took action against these effects by paying his employees about double the going wage—that is, he paid workers extra to tolerate boring and unsatisfying work. The L&T Company first tried simply to call the workers a team and pay them a team bonus, but that didn't work. Only when management allowed the workers to work as a team, to tackle work problems and make work decisions, did the company realize any positive effect. And that positive effect came about only when management became desperate enough to try it: when morale hit bottom, when turnover began to seriously interfere with getting the job done, and when productivity fell to disastrous levels.

In general, the most common reason that companies turn to teams is not to promote employee satisfaction or even to increase productivity. It is simply to try to do something about problems that are getting worse.

The classic teamwork redesign case is that of the Swedish auto maker Volvo. The Kalmar plant, in Sweden, was designed to use work teams to assemble major parts of a car, with each team managing its own work. The reasons Volvo made this major change were the same, in part, as those behind L&T's decision: absenteeism and poor productivity. At Volvo these problems were partly caused by (and partly a result of) rampant alcoholism. What's more, under Sweden's generous labor laws and agreements, workers received up to 90 percent of their pay whether they showed up for work or not!

Why does teamwork design help solve the problems we've described? The answer has to do with people's workplace needs. People need work that enables them to exert some control over their actions. They need work that provides a sense of completion and personal achievement. Moreover, human beings want work that involves some interaction with others, not as a diversion but in the context of doing their work. The traditional industrial assembly-line hierarchical bureaucracy fails all three of these tests, while teamwork design passes all three, explicitly or potentially.

Teamwork improves productivity, not just morale. That's because teamwork design builds greater flexibility into operations, allowing organizations to deal effectively with environmental pressures: market forces, customer demands, government regulations, and other factors that impinge on or impact operations. At the same time, teamwork design helps companies deal with internal problems. It gives team members more control over the work, so that when there's a problem, team members can quickly study and correct it. Under the old standardized assembly procedure, things that went wrong weren't always noticed, since workers were not supposed to think and solve problems. That's why American auto plants have traditionally required large areas to store autos that come off the line with defects.

Teamwork design may sound great, but does it really work? Well, from the 1960s through the 1980s, many American organizations began to redesign work on a team basis, just like L&T. Is the team approach the only answer a company will ever need? Perhaps not; consider what happened at L&T *after* the problems were solved.

Troubles in Toyland—Again!

The learning bonus arrangement that management developed and imposed was now an embarrassment. Semi-skilled workers in the paint room were earning more than skilled workers in other parts of the plant.

People were beginning to complain that this was unfair. And the extra production in the paint room was creating a pile-up in front and a vacuum behind. Workers in the wood room complained that they couldn't supply the paint room fast enough, while those in the finishing rooms were angry about the boxes of materials stacking up and making them look slow!

The engineers were unhappy because they thought they appeared to be fools, and they let the foreman know how they felt. And the superintendent was distressed that the plant's wage structure was being shaken up.

The L&T case illustrates what happens when successful "local" team change results in organizational disturbances. Organizations are social systems made of mutually dependent parts. A change in one part—even a change that part of the organization regards as very successful—may lead to severe problems in other parts of the system. What benefits one department or unit may not benefit the organization as a whole.

In Chapter Three we'll see what L&T did to address these new troubles.

3

The Team-Based Company

Once again the foreman called the consultant, explaining the new problems. "Are you satisfied with the paint room team's performance?" asked the consultant.

"Of course," replied the foreman. "It's just that now I've got all these other problems—and people—on my back."

The consultant said he sympathized, but reminded the foreman that it was the organization and operation of the paint room they had been looking at, not the rest of the plant.

"You have two choices," explained the consultant. "First, you can forget everything and go back to the way it was before you did anything. Of course, that'll be tough on the paint room workers. If it means going back to the old ways, I doubt many of them will want to stay, after their experience with the new system."

"So what's my alternative?" said the foreman.

"Simple. Set up the other departments, or sub-department work units, as teams, just like the paint room team. Let them have more of a say about their work, too. Then not only will the other units be able to keep up with the painters, but they'll probably be just as pleased."

To Team or Not To Team

The foreman asked the consultant to meet with him and the plant superintendent to talk the matter over. After reviewing the paint room team's performance and comparing it with that of the other units, the superintendent decided that maybe the consultant wasn't as crazy as he'd thought. The three held another meeting, this time with the 11 other foremen and department heads. Some were eager to try the new system; others were pessimistic, and a few were adamant in their refusal to even consider it. After further discussion, nine supervisors said they were willing to go ahead.

The superintendent addressed the two holdouts. "Guys, I know you have strong reservations, but I think we ought to give this a try," he said. "That's my decision, and I'll expect you to work cooperatively with our consultant and with every other supervisor to get this new system going."

Go Teams Go!

There was considerable commotion and confusion over the next week or two. But finally each unit or department was organized as a team, and each team had some real control over its own work. One of the two foreman opposing the new system quit at the end of the first month. He was replaced by an assistant who was as enthusiastic about the new ways as the old foreman had been against them. The other opposing foreman adapted.

Over the next year, performance in every unit went up. Wood room workers, for example, had no trouble keeping the painters supplied with primed parts, and the doll assembly teams no longer faced surplus boxes of painted heads and limbs, since their own productivity equalled—and sometimes exceeded—that of the painters.

In most cases, the improvements owed more to common sense than industrial engineering. The assembly team, for example, rearranged its work area so that parts had to be moved less often. One of the wood room workers, a natural craftsman, took it on himself to tutor the younger employees in the art of handling cutting tools. In a few cases, a team called on an engineer to evaluate whether a certain step was actually necessary. In many cases, it wasn't. Eliminating that step saved time and cost.

The plant superintendent, however, couldn't help feeling uncomfortable. He sensed something in the system was inherently unstable—and he was right.

Before we explore that point, however, let's take a closer look at why L&T accomplished what it did.

THE WISDOM OF TEAMS

Teams are designed to deal with three types of problems. We've already mentioned the first type: job design that fails to meet workers' needs to control, to achieve, and to work together.

The second problem is a lack of resources—equipment, materials, knowledge, and skills—needed to do the job. This problem results from the specialized-task/assembly-line type of organization, which we described in Chapter One.

Specifically, in a specialized-task/assembly-line organization, each person performs only a small and highly specialized task, with the tasks fitting together in a planned sequence. But what if someone in the line makes an error? Defective products result. What if someone can't keep pace? The whole process breaks down. In contrast, a team approach builds in flexibility. Some team members may check products to make sure all operations are done correctly, and errors can be traced to the source. If the source is a particular worker, the team can arrange to teach him or her how to do it right; or, if the person doesn't have the necessary ability, another team member can take over that aspect of the task. If, in the most likely of cases, the design of the work process is flawed, the team can identify and solve the problem by changing the way work is done.

What about the person who can't keep up with the pace? In a team design, another team member can simply trade places with that person. Alternatively, the team can rearrange task operations to turn team members' different skills into advantages instead of liabilities. In other words, the team is able to apply resources—especially human resources such as knowledge and skills—more effectively. Teams can apply the diverse knowledge and skills of team members to solve unexpected problems.

The third problem that teams address is the inability to take rapid action. This problem occurs in hierarchical bureaucracies that operate according to Fayol's scalar principle: One must always gain the approval of one's superior on important decisions and actions.

But what about problems and circumstances that require quick response—when there isn't time to go "up the line" for approval? Because a team's resources and skills are greater than those of any one individual, organizations can delegate more authority to teams, allowing them the option of taking action without strictly following the chain of command. Thus, team design enables organizations to deal effectively with problems that need to be addressed quickly.

In sum, teams provide organizations with a better way of satisfying human work needs and avoiding many of the problems characteristic of hierarchical bureaucracies and specialized assembly-line production. That's probably why they've become so popular over the past 20 years. Indeed, the movement toward teams largely came about in response to external pressures that made simple standardization unworkable.

However, as we saw at the L&T Company, teams can produce new problems as they resolve old ones. Changes in one part of the organization may require widespread changes elsewhere. Indeed, that's exactly what occurred at L&T—more than once! Look at what happened next.

The Triumph of Teamwork?

For several years things at L&T were looking good. Sales and profits went up as the company developed a reputation for high quality toys at reasonable prices. It was able to keep up with demand, too, so that distributors came to count on L&T for special and seasonal orders.

But eventually, and despite the continued demand for quality toys, business began to fall off. And this decline coincided with the development of problems between units and departments.

Troubles Again

The painters were now such a strong and cohesive work unit that members often spent time together off the job. But all was not perfect in the new team paradise.

The paint room team members, for example, complained that the wood room team wasn't providing enough materials for them to meet the demands of the doll assembly teams, especially since they needed to provide each of these assembly teams with a range of styles. The wood room team members explained the matter simply: management had told them to reduce production due to reduced demand.

The doll assembly teams complained that neither the paint room nor the wood room team seemed concerned about their need to fill several different production quotas for those dolls that were in demand. And some of the doll assembly teams even complained that other doll assembly teams were getting more work—and the opportunity for higher bonuses—than they were. Sometimes inventories of a high-demand product that a particular doll assembly team was working on would "disappear" mysteriously, only to be found in some storage area weeks later. And, as if that weren't enough, a team making wooden pull toys complained that the wood room team neglected their materials needs, and they demanded a special paint team to assist them in their work.

So, after having solved its original problem with a team, and its second problem with a team organization, L&T was once again confronted with a new problem. This time, the problem seemed directly attributable to the apparently successful new team organization. In the next chapter we'll see what happened.

4

The New Industrial Organization

Once again the plant superintendent turned to the consultant who had helped in the past, explaining the new problems of decreasing sales and increasing inter-team conflicts.

"Would you advise us to consider downsizing at this time?" he asked. "Our directors have suggested that given the changes in market demand, we should consider focusing on the products we're best known for, and reduce our work force and product line."

"I don't think that's really going to solve your problems," said the consultant.

"Then I'm not really sure what our problems are!" exclaimed the superintendent.

The consultant explained that he saw at least three problems. "The first is internal," he said. "The teams have become so strong, so 'team-focused,' that they really don't see what we used to call 'the big picture.' That is, they don't really focus on the needs of other teams, or on the whole product. Each team is consumed with its own work."

"That seems to fit," agreed the superintendent. "What's the next problem?"

"You're just producing the same things, year after year, and not even checking to see what your customers want. After all, your customers' needs may be changing. Your second problem is external: being out of touch with your market."

"And," said the superintendent, "the third?"

"The third is simply that the teams aren't getting any messages from customers, directly or indirectly. After all, if you expect to satisfy your customers, you'll need to use your teams to build into your products whatever it is your customers want. But you're not even asking, and the teams are busy trying to focus more and more on just their own teamwork."

The superintendent thought the consultant made sense. "What can we do?"

The consultant said the company needed to begin listening to its customers. "You need to learn what customers want," he said. "Some of your work team members could probably help you figure out how."

He went on to suggest that L&T needed not more teamwork, but more work across teams. "You've got to find ways to get customers' needs into the work of the teams," he said. "And you've got to get better work-related communication going between and among teams."

Just Among Us Teams . . .

The superintendent was puzzled; "How do we do it?" he asked.

"It's not easy," the consultant said. "The only way I know of is to use teams."

"But you just said we didn't need more teamwork!"

"This is a different kind of teamwork," explained the consultant. "You need to form a task force team composed of workers from different teams and supervisors from different areas. This team will be charged with identifying why your products aren't what customers want. That means team members will talk with customers, review sales charts, and look for as much hard data as possible to shed light on this problem.

"You also need to form some internal cross-function teams, to look at the problems and disputes between teams and work units. You might start with a cross-function task force team composed of people from the wood room, the paint room, the pull-toy unit, and several of the doll assembly teams. They could start by tracking the work flow and looking for the problems.

"Finally, you might consider forming a cross-function team composed of people from different teams and units who all work on one of your most important products. This team would look not just at each separate work process, but at how things all come together to make a high-quality, low-cost item that satisfies the customer. Some organizations have found it useful to make some of these product teams permanent; they've even redesigned the work itself around the new cross-function teams."

The superintendent found, however, that it was harder to create cross-function teams than it had been to create work teams in the first place. Many employees didn't want to work on a new team; they wanted to stick with the team they had.

Nevertheless, the external cross-function task force ultimately found out why a key product was no longer selling and what design changes were needed to turn things around in time for Christmas orders. The marketing manager reported that he knew this design change was needed, and he had sent around several memos—which apparently had been filed somewhere. But he hadn't pressed for the change because he assumed L&T's equipment couldn't handle it. The cutting room foreman set him straight.

During the following year, the problem-focused cross-function teams identified and resolved several inter-team problems that had been festering for a long time. And the year after that, L&T formed a permanent cross-function team to develop, design, and produce a new toy product for a market that the external cross-function task force had identified.

THE NEW INDUSTRIAL ORGANIZATION

Teams like those originally set up at L&T were designed to resolve old problems, problems that called for rapid and effective reactions. They're not irrelevant or unimportant, but organizations today face new problems, which teams may actually make worse. These new problems require a proactive rather than a reactive approach.

The problems that organizations face today fall into two groups. The first includes internal inefficiencies and conflicts produced by teams that are, by design, highly independent. Such independence may come at a high cost, if what's really needed is effective, proactive interdependence.

Consider again, for example, the classic case of Volvo. This manufacturer designed and institutionalized effective "semi-autonomous" teams, which worked more or less on their own on a particular assembly process or "chunk" of the job. Volvo's organization represents the "socio-technical systems" approach to work design. Its work teams represent the "joint optimization" of organizational and human needs.

The socio-technical systems approach involves analyzing the work process and redesigning the work so that teams can act as independently as possible. At Volvo, management accomplished this by "buffering" the semi-independent teams from one another. However, it then had to build extra inventory, so that teams would get neither ahead of nor behind one another and create larger problems. In this way, the socio-technical approach produces inefficiencies, reducing the value that team design adds. At Volvo, buffer inventories wasted resources and forced the company to use plant space—which might otherwise have been put toward productive ends—for storage.

In L&T's case, the socio-technical approach resulted in teams that became so independent, they no longer clearly saw their common mission. Thus they fought and competed, since the company had purposely minimized their need to cooperate. By failing to coordinate effectively, independent teams can spur inter-group conflicts that wipe out the added effectiveness of team operation.

The second category of problems that organizations today face consists of external pressures, such as the pressures of change, competition, and customer demands. Instead of helping the organization deal with such pressures rapidly and effectively, independent teams may become so insulated from external affairs that they resist change, ignore competition, and fail to listen to (let alone seek input from) customers. To respond rapidly and effectively to external pressures requires more than just effective teamwork. It requires planning across functions and developing linkages across teams.

Organizations today can't afford to waste productive capacity. Nor can they tolerate the conflicts over resources and actions that result when semi-autonomous teams fail to see and accept their larger organizational mission and shared purpose. Perhaps, worst of all, the danger of misreading and/or responding ineffectively to (or even ignoring) external pressures is not simply waste and inefficiency; it's the very real possibility of organizational failure.

In a sense, that's what happened at Volvo. When sales slowed in the early 1990s, top management closed the team-based Kalmar facility. After all, capacity had to be reduced, and the Kalmar plant was plagued by problems of efficiency and inter-team conflict. Rather than tackle the difficult new problems directly, Volvo opted simply to shut the plant down.

But closing down isn't an especially good solution to the new problems created in part by effective but independent teams and in part by increasing external pressures. A better approach is to integrate team activities across the organization's operations. Such cross-team coordination makes it possible for the organization to deal with the type of external pressures we've described.

In sum, meeting the demands faced by the new industrial organization means developing and promoting effective linkages across teams, and linking the teams to external concerns—especially customer desires. Such linkages are the basis of *cross-*

function teamwork. We will examine the nature and development of cross-function teams by looking first at some early versions, then at some current applications.

EARLY CROSS-FUNCTION ANSWERS: THE MATRIX AND THE TASK FORCE

In *matrix organization,* teams are assembled to carry out specific tasks or projects. The project may be relatively short term, requiring a few days' or months' work, or relatively long term, extending over a period of years. Team members come from functional "home" departments (design, engineering, research, etc.) so everyone has two bosses: the home department manager and the matrix team manager. The matrix approach might be called "rent-a-team."

In the 1960s, as part of the moon landing program, the National Aeronautics and Space Administration (NASA) spearheaded the first large-scale application of matrix organization. Because the organization's aerospace contractors faced work that was both technically complicated and relatively long term, NASA decided to bring specialized human resources together as a team to do a job; when the job was done, these individuals joined new task force teams. The idea behind the matrix is simple; it's the operation that's complicated.

Also during the 1960s, Rensis Likert, a social scientist who had designed and advocated a team-based organizational structure, expanded his team approach by defining the temporary cross-function task force. He said that temporary task forces should consist of members from several different teams, who would analyze a problem and make a report with recommendations. These teams would not normally produce a product or deliver a service; rather, they would serve as a temporary coordinating device. The external cross-function task force team that L&T used to explore customer needs is an example of Likert's cross-function task force.

Obviously the matrix team and the temporary cross-function task force are similar in composition but different in mission. The matrix team works to complete a task, either making a product or providing a service, while the cross-function task force generally develops a problem analysis and recommendation report. The matrix team will often exist for a relatively long period, perhaps even years, while the task force normally completes its work in a matter of days, weeks, or (at most) months.

THE NEW CROSS-FUNCTION TEAM

The cross-function team of today is not really a part of either the matrix organizational structure or the "overlapping group and link-pin" structure that Likert developed. Of course, it brings together people who must interact and bring their diverse knowledge to bear to accomplish a task; but while some employees bring technical knowledge and expertise, others bring specialized knowledge of functions or operations, such as finance, engineering, product development, or marketing.

Further, our new cross-function team is usually more than just a temporary task force. Its members don't just analyze problems and make recommendations; instead, they often design and implement solutions—and they are the "internal customers" who will put those solutions into practice. This new cross-function team is the kind of team that L&T eventually created and used to develop, design, and produce a new product.

When a product or a service changes (or must be changed), the new cross-function team may change, too. A new member with special expertise may join, as may someone who understands how a certain department operates, especially if that department must contribute to the design, development, and delivery of the new or altered product or service.

But why do organizations need such teams? Because it is no longer possible for them to coordinate and apply information and knowledge through rules and standardized procedures. Effective coordination depends on people coming together to share, exchange, and apply their diverse knowledge, experience, expertise, and skills. Let's look at an example.

DESIGN FOR MANUFACTURE AT AT&T

Cross-function teams are an important part of "design for manufacture," an approach to quality improvement that fosters new and more effective cross-function work relationships, especially between engineering and production units. In the traditional organization, an engineering unit might design a new product and then ship off the plans to the production division. The production unit is likely to encounter problems that engineering never considered, and solving those problems results in delays and added development costs. But in an organization that uses the "design for manufacture" technique, engineering and production form cross-function teams from the start. The teams work to develop a design intended to make production as easy as possible.

Bell Labs tried this approach in designing a new circuit board. Normally, Bell Labs' design work would take place in New Jersey; plans would then be sent to the assembly plant in Oklahoma, where production would begin and problems would be resolved as they were encountered. But under the new approach, the organization formed a team composed of engineers from both New Jersey and Oklahoma. This new cross-function team worked proactively, planning every detail rather than waiting for problems to appear. It anticipated many production problems that would have otherwise turned up later and cost much more to correct. Even more important, the overall quality of the product improved. Compared to a prior, similar project, the final testing unit had 60 percent fewer software errors.

BEYOND DESIGN FOR MANUFACTURE

The concept behind design for manufacture is simply that product planning and design must be closely linked to the manufacturing process. (Of course, design and manufacturing, as well as all other functional operations, must be based on an understanding of customers' needs.) The temporary cross-function task force that L&T used to design a new toy product was, in principle, no different from the cross-function team Bell Labs/AT&T used. The same is true of Chrysler's new auto design teams. By creating cross-function teams of marketing, design, engineering, and manufacturing personnel, Chrysler was able to cut more than a year off the design-to-production time of its new LH model, as well as produce a car that outside experts rate higher in quality than the company's earlier products.

The Chrysler example includes functions other than just design and manufacturing. In fact, design for manufacture is really just a relatively narrow application of cross-function teamwork. Some organizations not only include in their team structure most or all of the ordinary functions needed to plan, design, produce, and deliver a product or service; they also include suppliers and customers. For example, in 1988 Procter & Gamble was one of the suppliers that Wal-Mart approached to establish a "partnership" arrangement. P&G found this worked so well, it began developing similar partnerships with other retailer-customers, such as Kmart. It now has more than 120 such teams, including sales, purchasing, and data processing experts. In some cases, the retailer's cash register data go directly to P&G, which can then track inventory and automatically replenish stock.

THE FUTURE OF THE CROSS-FUNCTION TEAM

We've come a long way from the team of eight painters adjusting the speed dial on their production line of painted wooden toy parts. Doubtless some of them went on to become members, perhaps leaders, of new cross-function teams. The cross-function team concept is proving to be powerful in action. We have seen examples of how organizations can use them to design something as compact as a circuit board or as large as a new automobile. Cross-function teams make the matrix concept less of a two-headed monster and more of a pragmatic approach to operations. They may involve customers and suppliers as partners in the organization's work. They may be temporary task forces or permanent product teams. In any case, they are becoming more and more common, because organizations of all types are finding them versatile as well as powerful.

It should be clear that in creating cross-function teams, organizations must consider the specific need they want to address. Only with a clear purpose in mind can the organization determine whether such a team should be temporary or permanent, and which areas or functions should or must contribute members. Essentially, the purpose of the cross-function team defines its duration and form.

As with any tool, cross-function teams are effective only when the involved individuals have the necessary knowledge and skills. General knowledge can be conveyed through a briefing such as this one, but practical knowledge and skills are best developed through guided practice and experience. Part II of this briefing discusses some of the methods and techniques cross-function teams often find useful, and offers approaches for developing cross-function teamwork skills.

The Horizontal Organization

It had been a few years since the consultant had last heard from L&T when one day he received a call from the paint room foreman. "Not a new problem, I hope!" said the consultant.

"Well, not really . . . at least not like the ones we had to deal with in the past," said the foreman.

"By the way, I understand you're now supervising several teams, across functions. Is that part of the new problem?"

"Sort of," said the former paint room foreman. "You see, we found that we didn't seem to need so many supervisors, so when someone retired or left, we just assigned those supervisory functions to one of those remaining. At the end of last year we had four supervisors, not the eleven we started with."

"Then is your problem understaffing in management?" queried the consultant.

"Oh, no!" was the quick response. "Things work a lot better now that we've learned to use cross-function teams. We just don't need all those supervisors."

"Okay, I give up! What's your problem?"

"This month the plant superintendent retires. I've been asked to take on the job."

"Sounds like a nice promotion! What's the problem—don't you think you can handle it?"

"I think I can handle the job all right, not that I don't feel a little nervous. No, my problem may seem silly, but here it is: With all the changes around here over the past ten years, our old organizational chart doesn't bear much resemblance to the way things really work. But in looking it over I can't quite figure out what it *should* look like! I thought you might know of some models for organizations like ours."

"That's it?"

"There's one thing more. I can't even figure out what the job titles are of the supervisors and managers!"

The consultant was silent for a moment. "You know," he said, "some organizations have every person make up his or her own job title. The only requirement is that others understand what it means, with minimal explanation."

"That sounds like an idea worth trying. But what about the chart?"

"That's a lot more complicated. Why do you need a chart, anyway?"

"I just don't feel very comfortable. The organization's structure, without some sort of a chart, seems like it's just being constructed by the seat of the pants. But I know that's not really how things are. In fact, we're much *more* organized than we were before we started using cross-function teams."

"Don't your teams still have to analyze and modify work processes, on an ongoing basis?" asked the consultant.

"Of course," responded the plant superintendent-to-be. "Not to the extent we did the first year or two, but minor adjustments and improvements are being made constantly."

"Why then," suggested the consultant, "don't you have a temporary cross-function team, one with a member from every major functional unit in the plant, meet once a quarter, to review workflow processes and changes, and to update a complete workflow process chart?"

"But that seems to minimize the role of the managerial hierarchy," argued the superintendent-to-be. "Your chart would look a lot like a horizontal organization, with interdependent teams."

"Isn't the role of the managerial hierachy pretty minimal in fact?" asked the consultant. "And, hasn't L&T actually become a sort of horizontal organization, linked and integrated by cross-function teams?"

Now it was the new superintendent's turn to be silent. Finally he said, "I think you're right. I've been trying so hard to look back to what we were, that I've been ignoring what L&T has become. I'm going to try out your suggestions! Do you think you could help out?"

"I could, and it might be fun, but I really don't think you need my help. You've come a long way in the past few years, and I believe you can solve your own problems now. Why don't you set up a cross-function team, of the sort I suggested, and let them work it out. They should be able to apply my advice. Or, they might come up with better ideas of their own."

And that's exactly what happened.

Part II

Team Tools and Team Development

The two chapters in this section provide a foundation for helping members of a cross-function team "think together" and "work together" as they deal with workplace problems. Chapter Five presents a number of analytical tools that teams have found useful in understanding and improving workflow. Chapter Six addresses interpersonal and communication issues and suggests methods for helping members work together as a unit. Both sets of skills—analytical and interpersonal—are critical for effective cross-function work. The reader should realize that our list is far from complete and that our descriptions are necessarily brief. In every case, however, we provide one or more references for further study, for readers wishing to seriously consider how to go about creating and operating cross-function teams.

Part II

Team Tools and Team Development

5

Cross-Function Tools

Working effectively in cross-function teams calls for new methods. We describe those methods as "tools"—analytic approaches that can prove helpful in understanding and improving workflow within a function, or for gaining a clearer view of how work processes flow across functions.

Several of the tools described in this chapter are relatively structured, involving a series of step-by-step procedures. Others are less structured, with general guidelines rather than detailed start-to-finish instructions.

Our aim is to include only the tools we see as being of special, even crucial, importance for cross-function teams. Many other tools are also useful. An excellent general reference is *The Team Handbook,* written by Peter Scholtes and his associates and published by Joiner Associates in Madison, Wisconsin. Another helpful reference is *The Memory Jogger,* developed by Michael Brassard and published by GOAL/QPC in Methuen, Massachusetts. It's an inexpensive little booklet designed to fit in a shirt pocket, with clear step-by-step instructions for using the "seven old tools" of total quality management (brainstorming, Pareto charts, fishbone diagrams, scatter plots, and the like).

STRUCTURED TOOLS

1. Flow Charts

Flow charts, sometimes called *input-output charts,* give a visual description of the specific steps in a work activity or a series of activities. This can be extremely helpful for understanding exactly what is currently being done and then determining how to improve that process. To redesign a work process, the team can use two sets of flow charts: One shows what is *actually* happening, the other what *should* happen.

Flow charts use standard symbols to refer to certain types of activities. The most common and important are diamonds, which represent decision points; boxes, used to indicate work activities; and ovals, showing the start or stop points. But these conventions are not as important as getting down a clear description of the sequence of work activities and decisions.

Flow charting is especially useful for examining work activities that involve several teams or groups, that is, when coordination between and among groups is important. As work moves between functions, one group's output becomes input for another group. The second group's input (what it receives from the first group) usually has to meet certain requirements (e.g., of quality, quantity, timeliness, etc.). If this is not the case, then the second group's work may be disrupted or ineffective.

One of the first cross-function teams formed at the L&T Toy Company used flow charting to examine problems of coordination among the wood room, paint room, and assembly room teams. A temporary cross-function task force, consisting of the paint room foreman and a worker from the wood room, the paint room, and the assembly room, addressed this issue. The team developed a flow chart tracing the progress of toy parts from wood room to paint room to assembly room. (See Exhibit 5-1.)

By studying and discussing the flow chart, the cross-function team saw how the decisions made by the wood room team, concerning production scheduling for the various toys

Exhibit 5-1. A flow chart.

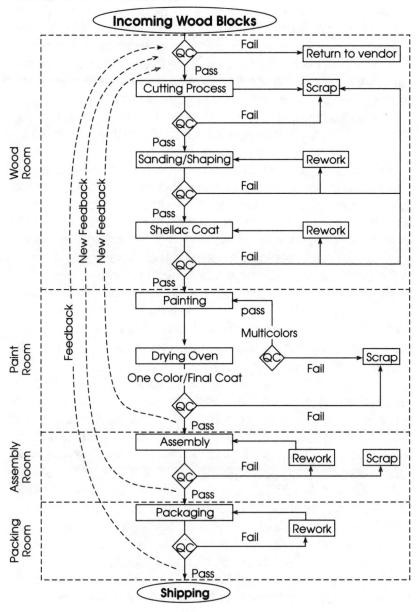

and parts, affected the paint room team. Recall that the paint room team could vary the speed of production, although this depended partly on the nature of the parts, since some (those with two or more colors) had to go through the drying oven more than once. The speed of the paint room team's production—and the choice of the sequence in which to paint various items—would then affect the assembly room teams, with some teams having too much to do and others too little.

The packaging room didn't have much trouble, but the feedback that this team relayed back to the wood room could easily mislead the wood room team. In other words, status reports from the packaging room might well suggest there were fewer (or more) of some toys being produced than the production plans given to the wood room called for. In fact, the surplus or deficit was often an illusion, due to changes in the work-in-process scheduling. For example, the paint room might have decided to deal with a large batch of multi-color parts. Or the assembly room might not have been able to deal with all of the paint room team's output of the parts for a particular toy. The wood room team would then make the problem worse by overproducing some sets of parts (to make up for an apparent deficit) and underproducing others (to "correct" an apparent surplus).

The task force addressed this problem by adding new feedback loops. Once the wood room knew more about the "time effects" of parts needing several colors, this team was able to schedule its activities so as to help the paint room team maintain a regular flow of product to all of the assembly room teams.

A second feedback loop established more timely and accurate communication between the assembly room and the wood room. Once the assemblers let the wood workers know their production status on a regular basis, the wood room team could set its production to keep pace.

All-in-all, the temporary cross-function task force was able to use the flow chart analysis to "smooth out" the production process and eliminate bottlenecks that had developed due to the lack of planned coordination among the teams.

2. PERT/CPM[1]

The acronym "PERT" stands for "Planning, Evaluation, and Review Technique," while "CPM" means "Critical Path Method." These are very similar approaches to graphically planning out each step in what is often a very long chain of activities. The focus of PERT is simply on describing each of the many specific actions that are the means to a goal. It was developed for the space program, when contractors had to plan and build extremely complex devices. By laying out the steps in complete detail, project managers at various levels could see exactly where the start of one step depended on effective completion of another, or where two activities had to coordinate before a third could be started.

Although developed independently, CPM is now almost always seen and used together with PERT. CPM identifies the "critical path," that is, the *longest* chain of events that is necessary to reach a goal. In most complex processes, several activities can occur simultaneously. If one wishes to reach the goal faster or more efficiently, then the way to do so is to redesign those activity segments that are critical (that are part of the longest chain of activities) and to run as many simultaneous activities as possible.

Because a PERT Chart shows specific activities and their outcomes in sequence, it is essentially a special type of flow chart. PERT Charts, however, generally use a less complex set of graphic symbols. The most common are *arrows*, which symbolize activities, and circles or *nodes*, which represent beginning and end points of activities. The diagram then shows clearly the way activities fit together. Most PERT users indicate a time for each activity, sometimes with "optimistic," "average," and "pessimistic" projections. These are not simply guesses; the

[1]A standard reference for PERT/CPM is *A Management Guide to PERT/CPM* (2nd ed.) by J.D. West and F.K. Levy (Englewood Cliffs, NJ: Prentice-Hall, 1977).

optimistic time estimate is the time an activity would take if everything went right. The pessimistic estimate assumes the worst possible scenario—a situation in which just about everything goes wrong. The "average" estimate is somewhere between these two extremes. When the PERT Chart is complete, with each activity, event node, and time estimate, it's possible to trace the critical path and find ways to reduce the time and cost associated with the activities in that path.

Let's return to the L&T temporary cross-function task force that used flow charting to deal with coordination problems.

While the flow chart exercise and new feedback loops made the coordination problems less severe, those problems were not eliminated. This is because flow charts give information only about the *sequence* of decisions and process activities. The *time* it takes to complete activities remains unspecified.

By reviewing the situation using PERT/CPM, the team was able to identify much more precisely the proportions of the various toys and parts that should be moved through the system for greatest efficiency.

Exhibit 5–2 shows the PERT/CPM chart they developed for this purpose. The greatest benefit of this analysis is that it helped the team see what trade-offs needed to be made when (as was usually the case) the demand for more of one product made it impossible to keep to a schedule of maximum efficiency. Later, a permanent cross-function team found PERT useful for planning and monitoring production of a new toy.

3. Variance Analysis[2]

Understanding and measuring variation is at the heart of total quality management (TQM) and of work process improve-

[2]A detailed approach to variance analysis can be found in the article "Analytical Model for Sociotechnical Systems," by Fred E. Emery and Eric L. Trist, which appears in *Sociotechnical Systems: A Sourcebook*, edited by William A. Pasmore and John J. Sherwood (San Diego: Pfeiffer & Company, 1978; pp. 120–131).

Exhibit 5-2. A PERT/CPM chart.

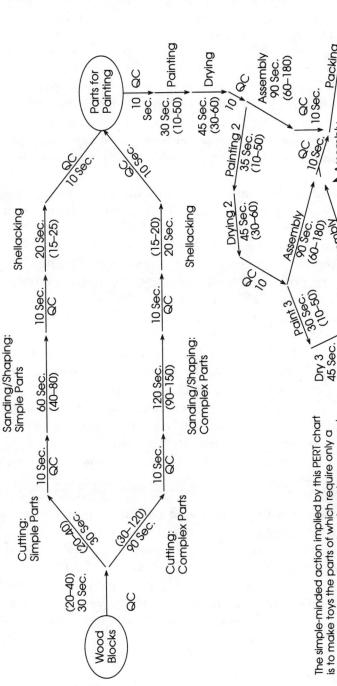

The simple-minded action implied by this PERT chart is to make toys the parts of which require only a single coat of paint. Examples of a serious approach are to (1) ask how to reduce the wood room time used to produce complex parts, (2) find ways to reduce drying time (especially for multi-color parts), and (3) design ways of partially assembling toys with multi-color parts; i.e., partially assemble these toys using one-color parts so that the multi-color parts can be added quickly when dry.

ment in general. Variance analysis is also basic to socio-technical systems design, which was mentioned earlier. All human activities (and all work activities) involve some variability. That variability can always be described statistically.

Variability can be reduced, sometimes to the point that it's not even measurable. In manufacturing operations, reducing variability is a crucial starting point for improving quality and ensuring product reliability. There are also countless applications in service operations, especially when important components of the service (accuracy, timeliness) can be easily measured.

But not all activities are equally variable. One must, therefore, study work processes to identify those activities with exceptionally high variability. What's more, it's not always true that high variability makes much difference. It's important to identify those work processes for which variability is high *and* for which this poses problems. For these situations, it's worth investing the time and effort needed to reduce variation.

Fred Emery and Eric Trist, social scientists who were instrumental in defining, developing, and applying the sociotechnical systems approach, suggest that the cross-function task force conducting a variance analysis be headed by the manager in charge of the process being analyzed. In addition, the task force should include representatives from various other groups that have some connection with the work process under study, along with whatever outside assistance is needed.

Emery and Trist identify four specific steps in conducting a variance analysis:

• *Step One: Identify all input and process variances.* List all variances arising from either inputs (raw materials as well as non-material inputs, such as information) or the design of the work process itself. This requires interviewing the managers, supervisors, and workers directly involved in the process under study. In addition, team members should draw on their background knowledge of "how things work" to identify inputs that those directly involved may have overlooked. Often, this step has to be carefully reviewed, sometimes repeatedly, to make sure that all of the variances have been listed.

• *Step Two: Connect variances with specific task activities.* The team does this by organizing the list to show those variances that relate to a specific part of the work. This helps to identify where feedback loops exist—or where they are needed, but *don't* exist. It also gives a clear understanding of where variations "cluster" in the sequence of task activities that make up the work flow. This helps in the next two steps.

• *Step Three: Identify key variances.* This calls for both data and judgment. Only persons well-acquainted with the work process are qualified to review the list and location of variances and develop an initial list of key variances.

• *Step Four: Review the list, evaluate the items, and make a final list.* The team now checks the tentative list developed in Step Three against four criteria:

(1) Does this variance significantly affect the quantity of production?
(2) Does this variance significantly affect the quality of production?
(3) Does this variance significantly affect operating costs (materials, labor, etc.)?
(4) Does this variance significantly affect "social costs." For example, does it place undue stress on workers, increase unreasonably the degree of task difficulty and effort required to do the work, or create unacceptable dangers to people's health and well-being?

Consider a very narrowly defined work process, the painting of wooden doll parts at L&T. The variability in the number of painted wooden doll parts produced depended on three key variances: variability in the rate at which the wood room team produced doll parts (an input variance), the rate at which parts were painted by the paint room team (a work process variance), and the variation in number of colors (coats) of paint per part (another work process variance).

Remember that the wood room team produced a number of parts other than those that were used to assemble dolls. By exercising control over their choice of which parts to produce, in terms of sequence and rate (that is, by controlling variability) the wood room team could better coordinate its output with the operation of the paint room team and the needs of the doll assembly teams.

Similarly, by specifically scheduling what parts to paint in what quantity—again, controlling variability—the paint room team was able to coordinate its output to better meet the assembly teams' needs. The final result was better control by the doll assembly teams over the quantity of product these teams turned out, and removal of a cross-function problem based (in part) on uncontrolled variation.

Variance analysis is often technically complex, and it can be quite costly. This is why it makes sense to look for (and try to control) only *key* variances, the ones that make a real difference. For example, it obviously takes longer to paint some toy parts than it does to paint others; the body of a toy truck takes more time to paint than does a doll limb. However, the actual time differences are so small as to be unimportant; the critical difference in painting time for different parts is due to multi-color parts that must go through the drying oven more than once. The paint room team's choice of speed of the paint line depends on the speed at which the team members choose to work, not on differences among parts. Thus, although there are such differences, they are ignored in variance analysis of this process.

Once a team has identified key variances, it may be a relatively simple matter to improve control. Or, it may require sophisticated and constant monitoring, as through the use of statistical process control charts. (GOAL/QPC's *Memory Jogger* shows how to construct SPC charts.)

SEMI-STRUCTURED TOOLS

1. Workflow Analysis [3]

The simplest part of workflow analysis is constructing a diagram showing how work actually (physically) flows from person to person, group to group, department to department, and so on, throughout the organization. If we tried to do this for all the work activities of the organization at once, it would quickly prove impractical because of the complexity involved. So, a workflow analysis must of necessity be limited, either to a part of the organization or to a specific work product (or service). Nonetheless, a clear visual picture of what actually happens to a part, a paper, or information can make inefficiencies and wasted efforts become obvious to everyone. In this respect a workflow analysis diagram is nothing more than another type of flow chart.

Exhibit 5–3 is a workflow diagram showing the making of a wood doll at the L&T Toy Company. The temporary cross-function task force team used this diagram to look at coordination problems among the wood room, paint room, and assembly room teams as they went about their specific tasks. The diagram reveals no major problems between or among the various teams. Still, it helped the cross-function team figure out that sorting the dry parts for a single toy into bins, with sub-bins for each part, and then placing the bins on wheels, would eliminate wasted efforts on the part of the assembly room teams.

It also showed that the repeat trips through the drying oven for multi-color parts created an imbalance in the number of painted parts available to assembly room teams working on a particular toy. Because some parts required only one color,

[3]This presentation of workflow analysis is based on material in *The Team Handbook* by Peter Scholtes and associates (Madison, WI: Joiner Associates, 1988; pp. 2–22 to 2–23) and on concepts developed by Pradip Khandwalla and detailed in Chapter 12 of his book *The Design of Organizations* (New York: Harcourt, Brace, 1977; esp. pp. 453–456).

Exhibit 5-3. A work-flow diagram.

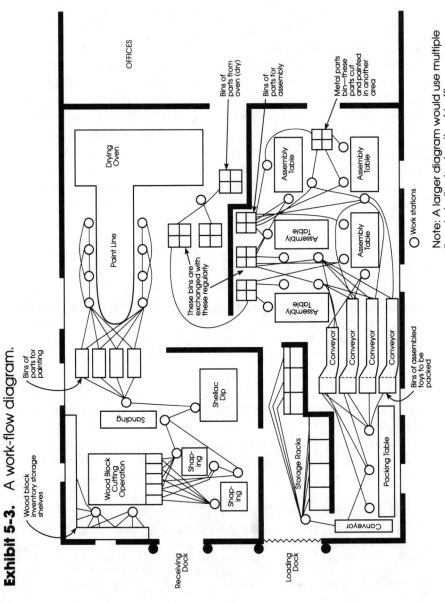

OFFICES

Drying Oven

Paint Line

Bins of parts from oven (dry)

Bins of parts for assembly

Metal parts bin—these parts cut and painted in another area

Assembly Table

Assembly Table

Assembly Table

Assembly Table

Assembly Table

These bins are exchanged with these regularly

Bins of parts for painting

Wood block inventory storage shelves

Sanding

Shellac Dip

Wood Block Cutting Operation

Shap-ing

Shap-ing

Storage Racks

Conveyor

Conveyor

Conveyor

Conveyor

Conveyor

Packing Table

Bins of assembled toys to be packed

Receiving Dock

Loading Dock

Note: A larger diagram would use multiple lines to indicate density of traffic.

◯ Work stations

these would arrive sooner and in greater quantity than the others. This led the paint room team to work with the wood room team to design an improved coordination process, to make sure that there would be enough finished and painted parts available to assemble the scheduled quantity of a particular toy, without waiting for more parts from the paint room.

While the aspect of workflow analysis just described is often quite valuable in itself, this tool achieves its greatest utility if the people using it pay simultaneous attention to three key dimensions of workflow: complexity, variability, and interdependence. There are few guidelines for preparing this sort of analysis, which combines both the physical mapping of workflow with an examination of its more fundamental dimensions. We will briefly explain the nature of each dimension.

Complexity. A workflow may be rather simple, calling for little search for information and infrequent problem solving. In this setting, workers rarely need to make "unusual" decisions. Again, consider the paint room at L&H Toys. Contrast this with the complex workflow in a hospital emergency room. This is the far end of the complexity spectrum—a setting that demands a great deal of information, continuous problem solving, and frequent departures from routine decision making.

The greater the complexity in a workflow, the higher the need for teamwork, since no one team member is likely to have as much expertise as is needed for dealing with a specific work problem. The greater the need for special kinds of expertise, the greater the need for some kind of cross-functional link.

Variability. The concept of variability here is a bit different from that described in variance analysis. Here we're speaking of the extent to which actions or steps in a work process do or do not follow a routine or prescribed pattern. Sometimes variability is very low, almost non-existent; workers repeat the same sequence of steps over and over and over. But it's also possible that each piece of work flowing through the unit calls for a very different set of actions.

A doll assembly team at L&T faced almost no variability in workflow, while the workflow through the paint room was moderately variable. At the extreme, a small unit of highly skilled craftspersons made the "dies" used to stamp out the few metal parts used in certain toys. These two workers had an extremely variable workflow, since most dies had to be custom designed and produced.

With high variability comes increased difficulty in planning and a greater need for high flexibility. All this calls for greater coordination than does the low-variability setting, for which a few standard sets of rules and procedures may provide adequate coordination across units.

Interdependence. A hospital operating room team is composed of highly interdependent personnel; this team, in turn, must depend on the efforts of teams and units external to the operating room. The demand for coordination is very high, and advance planning can play only a limited role. There is a need for real-time and rapid coordination of both information and materials available only through external teams.

Contrast this with the moderate degree of interdependence among the wood room team, the paint room team, and the various toy assembly teams. Problems among these teams can be avoided by advance planning and by designing inter-team feedback loops to provide the degree of immediate coordination needed. When problems occur, they can usually be resolved without extreme effort, if they are addressed promptly. It's even conceivable that a cross-function product team (like the one eventually developed) could combine all of the work activities required to produce a specific toy, with minimal need for coordination with any external units. In that case, there would be very little interdependence with other teams or units.

Applying workflow analysis. The three factors just defined—complexity, variability, and interdependence—are interrelated aspects of workflow. It should be obvious that greater complexity usually implies more variability as well as a higher degree of interdependence among work units contributing to the completion of a very complex task. But by breaking out these three factors, we can gain greater leverage over workflow problems and what to do about them. There is, however, no simple or clear set of steps that tells one how to do this; that's why we consider this tool "semi-structured."

In the case of the L&T Toy Company, we see that relatively low complexity might make for cohesive teams composed of members who can all carry out most or all of the tasks performed by the team. Variability is either moderate, for the wood room and paint room teams, or low for the assembly room and packing room teams. Interdependence among all the teams is moderate. This suggests exactly the sort of development we saw: a move from individual work to teams, followed by more and more independence of these teams from one another, to the point that coordination began to seriously suffer.

Even this brief a sketch of the workflow at L&T might have helped avoid the conflicts among highly autonomous work teams, had the analysis been done early enough. It would have pointed clearly to the need for additional feedback loops between and among teams, to enable better coordination.

That, of course, is exactly what the L&T cross-function task force concluded. Understanding the concepts just defined— complexity, variability, and interdependence—helped the team know what to look for in analyzing the flow chart the team developed. However, because it generally takes a cross-function team to carry out this sort of analysis, it's unlikely that knowledge of workflow analysis (on the part of the paint room foreman, for example) would actually have proved useful, even had it been available early on.

2. Differentiation/Integration Analysis [4]

This tool is based on the theory and research of two Harvard professors, Paul Lawrence and Jay Lorsch. Their work

[4]For more detail on this tool and its application see *Developing Organizations: Diagnosis and Action* by Paul R. Lawrence and Jay W. Lorsch (Reading, MA: Addison-Wesley, 1969).

centers on the idea that as organizations face new environmental challenges—new technology, increased competition, changing customer needs, etc.—they respond by "differentiating." This means that the organization creates new, specialized units to focus on and deal with the new problems. But greater differentiation makes it harder to "integrate," to pull the different parts back together into an effective and coordinated system.

Organizational units—work teams, departments, divisions, etc.—can be described in many different ways. Lawrence and Lorsch identify four variables on which differences among units are especially important: time orientation (short vs. long-term); goals; interpersonal style (informal vs. formal); and internal structure (number of levels, span of control, use of rules, use of control systems). When two units differ greatly on most of these variables, they are said to be highly differentiated.

The wood room, paint room, assembly room, and packing room at the L&T Toy Company all have clear and different goals—cutting and finishing wood parts, painting the parts, etc. All of these units, however, share a relatively short-term time orientation. While they might differ on the other two factors, formality and structure, there's no reason to believe that the four departments actually do differ in those respects. Thus, overall, we might say that differentiation is relatively low. Integration (effective coordination of inter-unit efforts) should, then, be relatively easy to attain.

However, the creation of a "paint room team" at L&T Toy Company differentiated this operation from the other work units. The paint room team became less formal, more like a friendly and cohesive group. The team began to think and plan its work over the entire day and not just from moment to moment. This newly increased differentiation, as we saw, created certain problems. Those problems were solved, initially, by differentiating the other units in the plant, i.e., by encouraging each unit to move to its own team structure.

When differentiation is high, there is clearly need for "integrative devices" to bring the units into a cohesive system.

The simplest such devices are rules (standard operating procedures) and paperwork communications. When differentiation is low, these simple tactics are likely to be adequate. But when differentiation is high, the organization needs more complicated devices. These include formal integrative roles, cross-function teams, and even integrative departments and units (whose defined full-time work is to coordinate and integrate diverse activities of differentiated units).

The development of new and more highly differentiated teams at L&T led to new problems, problems that Lawrence and Lorsch would label as issues of effective integration. The various teams became so independent that coordination began to seriously suffer. The new temporary and permanent cross-function teams were examples of Lawrence and Lorsch's integrative devices, designed to deal with the problems of increased differentiation.

While there is a series of steps to follow in applying differentiation/integration analysis, the specific actions are not well defined. Most steps ask questions that are not easy to answer in simple "yes" or "no" terms. Exhibit 5–4 outlines the five steps in using differentiation/integration analysis.

3. Affinity Diagrams[5]

The affinity diagram is somewhat unstructured in concept but usually well-structured in operation. The idea is based on early work by Richard Beckhard, a well-known organization development (OD) consultant who developed a technique he called "the confrontation meeting." This meeting involves many or most of the organization's members, coming together in one large room. Either in general session or subgroups, participants brainstorm and write down lists of problems, issues, and concerns. When the group has "run dry," the mod-

---

[5]This description of the affinity diagram is based in part on information in *The Memory Jogger Plus* by Michael Brassard (Methuen, MA: GOAL/QPC, 1989; Ch. 1, pp. 17–39).

Exhibit 5—4. Steps in Applying Differentiation/Integration Analysis

Steps in Application	Outcomes
1. Determine the nature of the environment: Is technology changing? How quickly? Is there much competition? Is it easy to get information?	Classify the environment as uncertain (changing), moderate, or certain (stable).
2. Examine the differentiated units in the organization and describe each in terms of the four characteristics: time; goals; interpersonal style; formal organization.	Compare the actual pattern of differentiation with the pattern that would be "best" as determined by the nature of the environment.
3. Describe the integrative methods being used, especially within, between, and across units for which integration is important.	Compare the actual pattern of integrative activities with the pattern that would be "best" as determined by the nature of the environment. Is the actual pattern too complex, adequate, or inadequate?
4. Describe how conflicts are managed. Is conflict usually hidden or smoothed over? Do conflicting parties fight it out? Are conflicts openly faced as problems to be mutually resolved?	If conflicts are not openly faced and dealt with as problems, then people in those organizational units not using this approach need to develop new skills in managing and resolving conflict.
5. Determine what new integrative methods are needed, if any.	Put into use new integrative methods, if needed.

erator reviews the lists, and with participants' involvement, organizes the specific items around common central themes to define problems. The group may then prioritize the problems and proceed to work on the most important ones. More often, the group creates task forces charged to study specific problems and come back with recommendations.

The affinity diagram is no more a diagram than the confrontation meeting involves a confrontation. And while the number of people involved is usually small (just three or four to as many as ten people), the activity is much the same as that developed by Beckhard. One difference is that rather than brainstorming problems and issues in general, the group starts with a defined problem area in which to work.

Once the problem area is defined, the group begins to brainstorm, either privately or as a group. Sometimes ideas are written privately on index cards, rather than posted on newsprint, to make it easier for the group members to share even strange or unusual ideas. On the other hand, the use of flip charts so that everyone can see each idea written as it is stated may help stimulate others to come up with additional ideas. When the group members have generated as many ideas as possible, the group works to sort them into categories, just as is done in a confrontation meeting. Everyone participates in sorting the ideas into a number of groups (ideally between six and ten). (Sometimes a few ideas don't fit any category; these are simply set aside.) This is a very unstructured process that continues until everyone is satisfied with the way the ideas have been sorted.

Next the group discusses the content of each category, one at a time, to come up with a theme or label. Finally, the ideas in each group are put together on a chart, under common themes. The chart, and the ideas, can then be shared with others; work can begin on using the ideas to address and solve the problem.

The external cross-function task force formed at L&T Toy Company used an affinity diagram to address the issue of under-

Exhibit 5-5. An affinity diagram.

WHAT DO OUR CUSTOMERS WANT?

Feel Good About the Purchase/Product		Physical Appearance Factors		Design Considerations		
VALUE	**SATISFACTION**	**STYLE**	**QUALITY**	**RELATED PRODUCTS**	**VARIETY**	**AGE-APPROPRIATE**
Items can be purchased individually, not just as a set, so even though prices are not low, items are affordable.	Children enjoy playing with the toys.	Traditional wood construction.	Non-toxic paints.	Lines of products with common themes (cars, boats, etc.)	Different product lines.	Different toys in the same product line are aimed at specific different age groups.
Items can be added one-by-one to make larger sets.	Children form strong attachments to specific "favorite" toys.	Current, not "old fashioned" subjects (cars, trucks, etc.).	No sharp edges; smooth surfaces.	Items from different product lines relate (e.g., dolls that can ride in cars).	Varied toys within a product line.	As a child grows, new toys are available that are familiar (due to relatedness of design), but more "advanced."
Quality justifies price points.	Parents feel good about toys' value.	Design must be aesthetically pleasing.	Colors are bright.	Similarity among product lines in feel, color, sizes, etc.	Toys are designed for children of different, varied ages.	Complexity is added for older children by expanding the number of items in a set and the way those items interrelate (not just by having more complex items)
Toys' permanence adds to value.	Toys hold children's interest.	Toys remind parents of toys they played with as children.	Handcrafting is evident.	Items within a product line have good fit with one another.	New items are developed regularly, added to existing product lines.	Products cover a wide range of age groups.
	Children look forward to getting new items in a set due to satisfaction with items they have.	Items have a degree of sophistication; not seen as "crude."	Toys are durable, don't break easily.	New items are designed to fit well with older items in a product line.	Toys targeted for girls, for boys, or for both.	
		Toys have solidity—weight, physical substance.	Toys can be repaired if damaged.	Items in a set promote cooperation among several children.		
		Toys are true to form of objects represented; not unrealistic.	Paint doesn't chip or peel.			
			Toys perform as intended.			
			Paint doesn't fade.			
			No defects.			

standing customers' needs. After conducting customer interviews and focus group meetings, the six task force members (including a manager, an assembly room team worker, a paint room team worker, a wood room team worker, a person from the marketing staff as well as the buyer for a major toy store chain) reviewed various industry reports and analyses. Finally, they met to use their information to develop an affinity diagram. Their problem definition was, "What do our customers want?" Using a flip chart and a brainstorm process, the team developed a list of 68 items, with some repetition and overlap. A quick overview showed that there were 41 different items. The team members then discussed these items and sorted them into seven categories; this took some time until everyone was satisfied. Finally, there was a discussion of each category and the team decided on a label for each. Their final affinity diagram is shown in Exhibit 5–5.

THE LIMITS OF TOOLS

When properly applied in appropriate circumstances, the tools described here, along with others, can be of great use in helping to define and solve cross-function problems. As team members become familiar with and more skilled in the use of these tools, it is less and less important to carefully follow the structured steps; using these types of tools becomes second nature.

But no tool or set of tools can substitute for the interpersonal cooperation, and expert communication skills needed to carry out a complex operation. Of course, no one starts out with perfect cross-function teamwork skills. Indeed, tools and good instructions in the use of tools serve as a starting point for skill development. But for members of different functions to work together as a team demands going beyond the kind of tools described in this chapter. Chapter Six describes methods that can prove useful in this regard.

6

Developing
Cross-Function Teams

In this chapter, we describe three methods for developing effective cross-function teams and helping team members acquire needed skills. Two of these methods have been around for many years; the third, "dialogue," is quite new. But all three can help an organization's cross-function teams work better and be more effective with the tools described in Chapter 5.

DEVELOPING INTERGROUP UNDERSTANDING[1]

Structured methods for helping group members work well together have been around since the 1960s, and today's approaches are not all that different. Perhaps the classic method was developed by Robert Blake, Herbert Shepard, and Jane

[1]Our description of this approach comes from the original work of Robert Blake, Herbert Shepard, and Jane Mouton, which is reported in their book *Managing Intergroup Conflict in Industry* (Houston: Gulf, 1964). See also *Team Building: Issues and Alternatives* (2nd ed.) by William G. Dyer (Reading, MA: Addison-Wesley, 1987; Chapter 11).

Mouton to help two teams resolve conflicts between them. Their technique consists of four steps.

First, the two groups meet separately, with each developing a detailed list of the problems it has with the other. Then each group (still meeting separately) tries to predict what problems will appear on the other group's list. This exercise can be fun, and it can also be a true learning experience, especially during the next step of the process.

In the second step, the groups present their lists to one another. First, Group One displays its list of problems. Group Two's members can neither object nor defend their positions. They can, however, ask questions of clarification. Next, Group Two gets its turn, while Group One refrains from arguing. Finally, each group presents its predictions, comparing these with the actual list. Most often, groups find that while they accurately predicted some of the other group's problems with them, they greatly overstated others.

Step Three calls for open discussion of the problem lists, with group members ultimately merging them into a single list that everyone can accept. This process may take a while; a good consultant or group facilitator can serve a useful role. If the problems are hard to define or have a long (and perhaps bitter) history, the exercise may simply stop with each group developing a "picture" of the other group that the other group accepts. Then each group convenes privately to discuss the differences of opinion between the two groups. Eventually, they meet together again to try to resolve those differences and come up with a single problem list.

Step Four begins once there is a single, agreed-upon list. The groups rank the problems and form cross-team subgroups to work on each one.

At L&T, the consultant used this four-step process to help teams with serious problems learn to work together more effectively. For example, a pull-toy assembly team and the paint room team used the four-step process to attack a problem that had been simmering for several months. The pull-toy assemblers had complained to the superintendent about the need to work overtime, and placed the blame squarely on the painters' "incompetent scheduling." This caused rumors to fly, giving the impression that the two foremen had "personal vendettas" against each other.

The first two steps of the process proved the rumors to be unfounded, and the two teams learned that they actually had a great deal of respect for each other. The problem, basically, was an inconsistent flow of painted parts, so that the pull-toy assemblers' productivity was often limited. By fine-tuning the production of painted pull-toy parts, the paint room team was able to smooth out the flow of parts to the pull-toy assembly teams without adversely affecting the work of other assembly teams.

The four-step process was also used by the consultant to help kick-off new cross function teams. In some cases, they started as task force sub-groups assigned to work on a particular problem identified in the four-step processes.

That's what happened when a cross-function task force was formed with members from the wood room team, the paint room team, and two doll-assembly teams, following a four-step process involving all four teams. The temporary cross-function task force team met to work on the problem of multiple product production quotas, but ultimately became a permanent cross-function team that met regularly to monitor the process and plan needed adjustments.

ROLE NEGOTIATION AND RENEGOTIATION

It's important that teams agree on what role each member will play. In establishing these roles, most teams find themselves moving through four phases.

First, members begin sharing information, which leads to the development of specific expectations. Next, each party makes a personal commitment to these roles and role expectations.

Phase Three is a period of stability. People perform the

roles they have taken on, which leads to productivity and confidence. But no matter how well-defined, clear, and accepted the roles and role expectations are, changes will inevitably occur as a result of external pressures or choices made by one party or another.

Thus, in Phase Four, role expectations are disrupted, creating uncertainty and uneasiness, anxiety and resentment, and often, finger-pointing.

This theoretical framework comes from John Sherwood and John Glidewell,[2] who suggest that at this point, the relationship can change in any of four ways. The parties can simply terminate their relationship, although in work settings this is usually impossible. A second option is a stalemate with disruptions continually occurring. Because this choice often produces stress, it's not likely to work over the long term.

Alternatively, the parties can return to the way things were and recommit to the old role definitions, although this choice does nothing to alter the factors that caused disruption in the first place. This means that further disruptions are likely, and each will be worse than the last. Finally, the parties can go back to square one, sharing new information and renegotiating role expectations.

It may seem as though Sherwood and Glidewell are advocating renegotiation. Actually, they recommend none of the options. Instead, they suggest the parties become sensitive to this pattern—that they recognize such phases are likely to occur. By learning to forecast and openly discuss changes in the workplace that are likely to affect their alliance, they are better able to deal with the disruptions. They can then decide whether to terminate their relationship, renegotiate their expectations, or try to remove the effect of the change, so they can maintain their stable and productive Phase-Three relationship.

Clearly, this model helps explain disruptions at the L&T

[2]John J. Sherwood and John C. Glidewell, "Planned Renegotiation: A Norm-Setting OD Intervention." In J.E. Jones and J.W. Pfeiffer (Eds.), *The 1973 Annual Handbook for Group Facilitators.* San Diego, CA: Pfeiffer & Company, 1973.

Toy Company. When the consultant recommended that cross-function teams be developed, he was drawing on this very process.

While Sherwood and Glidewell offer a simple but powerful model of how mutual expectations are set and changed, they provide no suggestions on how to develop this greater sensitivity and use it to plan renegotiation meetings. Roger Harrison,[3] however, provides a structured, five-step approach to conducting specific negotiations over mutual expectations.

Harrison's framework begins with discussion among the consultant and the parties. This prepares the parties to work together, to develop trust in the consultant, and to warm up to the task. In Step Two, the parties develop a contract, which is often written. Harrison says the following points are helpful:

- The consultant does not probe for feelings. After all, the subject is work relations and expectations, and how people feel is their own business. However, if the parties want to share their feelings, they can.
- The parties are expected to talk openly and honestly about their work and their expectations of one another at work.
- All expectations must be written down, and must be understood (although not necessarily accepted) by both parties.
- The sharing of expectations is just the beginning; changes occur only after the parties negotiate and reach agreement.
- The process of change is based on bargaining and negotiation; it is complete only after an explicit, detailed agreement is reached and put in writing.
- While the parties may negotiate using threats and pressures, they should realize that an excessively negative

[3]Roger Harrison, "Role Negotiation: A Tough-Minded Approach to Team Development." In W.G. Bennis, D.E. Berlew, E.H. Schein, and F.I. Steele (Eds.), *Interpersonal Dynamics*. (3rd. ed.). Homewood, IL: Dorsey, 1973.

approach often produces defensiveness, concealment, reduced communication, and efforts to get back at the antagonist. It may also lead to a breakdown in negotiations.

In Step Three, the parties and the consultant reach an understanding of how work actually gets done. Harrison offers a variety of structured activities to help each party do this, including:

- List the major types of decisions made, and identify who makes them.
- Identify who has influence over each type of decision.
- Draw an organizational chart that shows how often communication takes place between the parties and who typically initiates contact.
- Determine whether the current organizational structure is appropriate by relating it to the work flow and decision-making processes.
- Consider what changes should be made: What should the other party do more of, less of, or better? Also, what should not change?

The parties write down their responses to the activities above and share them with the group. People may ask for clarification of various points, but no arguments or discussions take place at this time.

Step Four consists of the actual role negotiation. The parties select issues to negotiate, while the consultant encourages negotiations of the sort, "If you do X, then I'll do Y." All agreements are put into writing. The process continues until all negotiable issues have been covered.

The fifth and final step is the follow-up. The parties adjourn to test their agreements, then meet again to review results and renegotiate agreements that are not working. As groups repeatedly go through this role negotiation exercise (due to ongoing changes that affect their relationship), they generally find that the process becomes easier, and they bring fewer and fewer problems to their follow-up meetings.

Harrison points out two problems with role negotiation. First, there's the possibility that the parties may bargain in bad faith; second, the external pressures that produced the need to negotiate may (and probably will) continue to change, so the new agreement eventually will work no better than the old one.

Both the Sherwood/Glidewell and the Harrison models apply most directly to conflicts between individuals and within teams, rather than to inter-group or cross-function team development. Nevertheless, these two methods can be applied just as well to situations involving two or more teams, or a single cross-function team whose members need to work together more effectively.

DIALOGUE: RESTORING BASIC COMMUNICATION[4]

Picture a group of people talking openly with one another and creating a free flow of meaning. If the participants had any "axes to grind," these were checked at the door, along with badges and other symbols of rank and authority. People are speaking as colleagues, and they feel confident they can raise sensitive issues or challenge one another's assumptions without rancor.

This is what Peter Senge and his colleagues, building on the writings of Martin Buber (the Austrian-born philosopher) and David Bohm (the British physicist) mean by *dialogue*. Senge notes that dialogue is different from discussion. In discussion (the root of the word suggests a "shaking apart") people are more or less "throwing" ideas at one another. In contrast, the

[4]Peter Senge's *The Fifth Discipline* (Doubleday, 1990) provides basic discussion of the dialogue method. The steps for conducting dialogue are based on articles by Edgar Schein and William Isaacs in the Autumn 1993 issue of *Organizational Dynamics*. The authors express their thanks to Don Bohl of the AMA staff for drafting the material in this section, and to Robert M. Fulmer for his thoughtful review and comment.

Greek roots for dialogue, *dia* and *logos,* suggest "meaning flowing through," a much deeper type of communication.

We have all experienced this kind of meeting-of-the-minds at some time in our lives, perhaps during a one-on-one session with a trusted confidant, a parent, or a spouse. But does a team really need to aspire toward this "higher plane" of communication? Perhaps not. Perhaps there's already a strong rapport among team members, to the point that they can challenge each other's assumptions, confront past failures without placing blame, and otherwise navigate through the political terrain without setting off land mines.

On the other hand, we are all human. Some of us have turf to protect and come to the table with our own agendas, our own identities as part of a department, and our own notions of what should be done. When challenged we may become defensive, pull rank, or place blame. Defensiveness puts a stranglehold on collaboration. Participants are caught in a bind: Raising sensitive issues and speaking their minds might move the group closer to its goal; just as likely, however, confronting the issues could cause polarization.

In such cases, dialogue provides a remedy. Although no one has yet developed a step-by-step manual for teaching people how to use the dialogue process for group and intergroup development, the basic principles are clear, and some of the commonly used techniques can be described. Following is a five-step outline of a typical dialogue process.

1. Group members must sit in a circle; there must be a sense of total equality.

2. The consultant or facilitator starts by asking group members to recall a time when they reached a "deeper" level of communication with another person. Each person then describes that event to his or her neighbor.

3. The facilitator asks the group for terms that describe this kind of talk. How does it differ from "normal" conversation? The facilitator lists these attributes on a flip chart. The list becomes the group's definition of "dialogue."

4. The dialogue begins with the facilitator going around the group, asking each person to tell what is on his or her mind. The first sessions have no set agenda; everyone must be given "air time." This is called "check-in," and its purpose is to build alignment within the group.

5. At some point, the facilitator explains several fundamental concepts, discussed below. The timing of this depends on what state the group is in and how ready it is to deal with new concepts. Let's look at two of these dynamics:

Key Dynamics: Suspension. As the talk continues, it's quite likely that someone will say something that another person finds threatening or distressing. Rather than striking back, demanding an explanation, or feeling hurt and retreating, the offended person should suspend any response. This doesn't mean ignoring the situation or repressing one's feelings; rather, it means creating a special "mental hook" on which the offending remarks and the feelings they provoked can be "hung out to dry." Often, as the dialogue continues, the offended party will realize that his or her reaction was based on a misinterpretation.

Key Dynamics: Listening for your own biases. Most training in interpersonal communication ("active listening," for example) attempts to help people focus on what other people are really saying. In dialogue, however, participants listen to themselves—to the biases or assumptions that arise in their minds when someone else is talking. The question is not so much, "What is this other person really saying?" as it is, "Why am I feeling and reacting this way to what that person said?"

After a number of open-ended sessions, the group can set its agenda and begin to work toward an objective. The facilitator may need to continue giving the group some guidance, for example, by asking participants to explore the assumptions behind a particular position.

If the group reaches a roadblock, the facilitator may draw a "map" of the psychological dynamics involved. This diagram might show, for example, the various positions people have taken, the assumptions behind those positions, the way different people responded to each position, the result of such responses, and so on.

Exhibit 6–1 shows such a map, based on a dialogue project led by William Isaacs of MIT. Isaacs was working to ease a longstanding deadlock in a Midwestern steel mill's union-management dispute. The arrows in the middle of the map show the "rut" union members had worked themselves into: Management's effort to "speak out" or "talk straight" was interpreted as "an attack of the same old kind." One response to this was to "go ballistic," which led to mutual bewilderment and withdrawal. The phrases at the corners of the map state the assumptions that were working on both sides.

Exhibit 6-1. A conflict map.

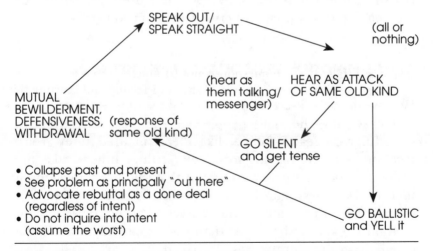

(Sound as if)

- See problem as principally "out there"
- See self as efficient, others as inefficient

- Present problems AND SOLUTIONS as done deal; do not inquire; do not make reasoning explicit
- Bypass joint problem identification

SPEAK OUT/
SPEAK STRAIGHT

(all or nothing)

MUTUAL BEWILDERMENT, DEFENSIVENESS, WITHDRAWAL

(response of same old kind)

(hear as them talking/ messenger)

HEAR AS ATTACK OF SAME OLD KIND

GO SILENT and get tense

- Collapse past and present
- See problem as principally "out there"
- Advocate rebuttal as a done deal (regardless of intent)
- Do not inquire into intent (assume the worst)

GO BALLISTIC and YELL it

Source: William N. Isaacs, "Taking Flight: Dialogue, Collective Thinking, and Organizational Learning," *Organizational Dynamics*, Vol. 22, No. 2 (Autumn 1993).

Isaacs reports that the dialogue participants learned to point to the map in the middle of a session and say, "We're falling back into the same old trap." This helped them back off from an impasse and talk through the issue from a different starting point.

Eventually dialogue participants create what Senge and Isaacs call a "container," that is, a "space" in which "hot" emotional issues can be placed without anyone getting burned. The result is a "safe" or "cool" form of communication, with people maintaining awareness of biases and formerly hidden assumptions, and working together toward a common goal.

Because members of a cross-function team usually have greater differences of perspective than members of traditional teams, the dialogue process can be of special benefit in developing cross-function teamwork skills. It's quite likely that each member of such a team has different assumptions about the business and a few defensive routines at the ready. Some practice in suspension and bringing assumptions to the surface will likely improve team efforts. Thus, dialogue might well prove valuable for working on difficulties between and among cross-function teams. It is probably most useful, however, for the ongoing development of cross-function team skills.

CROSS-FUNCTION TEAM DEVELOPMENT METHODS

We have described several methods and techniques for teaching and practicing the skills people need to work effectively in cross-function teams. Some, like the structured inter-group meeting, are old friends in a new setting; others, like the dialogue process, are new inventions that will take some getting used to. Doubtless, more such methods will be developed. But overall, we must remind the reader that no development method is likely to be better than on-the-job training. To the extent that the approaches described here are used in an artificial "training" setting, they will be weakened; if they are applied in the context of real cross-function teamwork, they will prove more powerful. About all that's certain is that cross-function teams will be an integral part of the twenty-first century organization. Those organizations that learn to use cross-function teams now will have a head start.

Conclusion

In this briefing we have covered the need for and the development and application of cross-function teams. We began with the development of the team approach, looking at where teams came from and how they work. We demonstrated how the initial, tentative use of teams evolved into the team-based organization. Finally, we saw how the team-based organization is being replaced by the horizontal organization, designed around cross-function teams that are composed of individuals from diverse areas, operations, and functions. As interdependencies expand, not just within the organization but to suppliers and customers, we are likely to see more and more uses of cross-function teams.

Boeing is spending more than $10 billion to develop its new wide-body 777 aircraft, which will sell for about $130 million per plane. For the first time ever, the company brought together temporary cross-function teams that included representatives of its customers, for example United Airlines, Japan Air Lines, and British Airways; machinists who worked on ground repair crews; maintenance staff who cleaned planes between flights; and pilots, flight attendants, and even passengers. The

777 design incorporates not just the desires but the problem-solving advice of individuals from all of these groups.

Flight attendants made a number of suggestions for redesigning the galley arrangements so they would be more efficient and easier to use. Pilots helped alter the cockpit layout. The mechanics had a latch redesigned so it could be opened by a person wearing gloves (a similar latch on 747s is so small, it can be opened only with one's bare fingers, and this sometimes results in fingers freezing to metal in icy winter weather). All in all, over 1,200 design changes were made on the basis of cross-function task force analyses and reports. Boeing expects this new flagship craft to compete successfully with the Airbus A340 well into the 21st century.

Cross-function teams are not a magic solution to organizational problems. Indeed, neither are teams themselves. Certain types of work will always be the province of the individual, while other tasks will continue to be done by "traditional" teams. But as we approach the next century, one thing is relatively sure: Most of us will probably be working in or with a cross-function team.

About the Authors

Marshall Sashkin holds a bachelors degree in psychology from the University of California, Los Angeles, and a doctorate in organizational psychology from the University of Michigan. He has taught at several universities and is currently professor of human resource development at the George Washington University. For several years, he held a special appointment to the U.S. Department of Education's Office of Educational Research and Improvement, where he developed and guided applied research aimed at improving leadership and organization in schools. He consults with organizations such as TRW, General Electric, Sara Lee, and American Express on issues of leadership, culture, and quality. More than 50 of his papers on leadership, participation, and organizational change have been published in academic journals, and he is the author or co-author of more than a dozen books, including two AMA Management Briefings. His most recent book is *Putting Total Quality Management to Work,* written with Kenneth Kiser (San Francisco: Berrett-Koehler, 1993).

Molly G. Sashkin earned a bachelors degree in history and English and holds two masters degrees, the first in secondary education and the second in guidance and personnel services. She has teaching experience at every level of the educational system, from preschool through elementary, secondary, and college levels. Molly's technical background includes the administration and interpretation of psychological tests and the development of job skills tests. She has been an academic adviser to the U.S. navy, a test development specialist for the U.S. Army, and a career development counselor for the U.S. Department of Commerce. She is a partner in Marshall Sashkin & Associates, a management and organization consulting firm, where she is responsible for the development, publication, and distribution of materials for management and organization development. Her recent consulting assignments include work with the World Bank on performance appraisal and with a local government on TQM.

For additional copies of *The New Teamwork: Developing and Using Cross-Function Teams,*

Call: 1-800-262-9699   OR

Write to: AMA Publication Services
            P.O. Box 319
            Saranac Lake, NY 12983

Ask for **Stock #02353XTEM.** $12.50 per single copy / AMA members $11.25 per single copy. Substantial discounts for bulk orders (11 or more copies).

OTHER AMA SPECIAL COLLECTIONS ON TEAMWORK

Building a Winning Team: High Performance Through Teamwork

This collection from *Supervisory Management* has 17 selected readings, 15 case studies, and 15 self tests with solutions. Are you a born leader? Don't worry, most of us aren't—we've had to learn how to be a leader. Turn your coworkers into **Team Members** and yourself into a greater company asset.   **Stock #06037XTEM,** $29.95 / AMA members $26.95.

Self-Managed Teams: Creating the High-Performance Workplace

Here are 8 articles from *Organizational Dynamics* to help you meet today's challenges. This collection provides you with an understanding of what it is like to make a transition to self-management, the demands placed on team leaders, the questions that employees raise, and the kind of organizational structure the approach demands. **Stock #06710XTEM,** $24.95 / AMA members $22.46.

Please complete the **ORDER FORM** on the following page and we'll rush your copies to you. Our Fax is: (518) 891-0368.

AMERICAN MANAGEMENT ASSOCIATION

PERIODICALS ORDER FORM

Rush me my Collections.

☐ Stock **#06037XTEM**

Building a Winning Team: High Performance Through Teamwork
($29.95 per copy, $26.95 per copy for AMA Members)

☐ Stock **#06710XTEM**

Self-Managed Teams: Creating the High-Performance Workplace
($24.95 per copy, $22.46 per copy for AMA Members)

Name: _____

Title: _____

Organization: _____

Address: _____

Phone: _____

Signature: _____

Please add appropriate sales tax and include $3.75 for shipping and handling.

☐ Payment enclosed

☐ Bill me

AMA's No-risk Guarantee: If for any reason you are not satisfied with any product we will credit you toward another product of comparable price or refund your fee. No hassles. No loopholes. Just excellent service—that's what AMA is all about.

American Management Association
Attn: Publication Services
P.O. Box 319
Trudeau Road
Saranac Lake, NY 12983